365 Mindful Days to Colour

First published in the UK in 2016 by
APPLE PRESS
74–77 White Lion Street
London N1 9PF
United Kingdom

www.apple-press.com

Copyright © 2016 Quantum Books Ltd

All rights reserved. No part of this publication may be reproduced or distributed in any form or by any means (including electronic, mechanical, photocopying, recording or otherwise) without prior written permission from the publisher.

QUM3DTC

This book was designed, conceived and produced by
Quantum Books Ltd
6 Blundell Street
London N7 9BH
United Kingdom

Publisher: Kerry Enzor
Managing Editor: Julia Shone
Editorial: Philippa Davis and Nicky Hill
Design: Amazing 15
Production Manager: Zarni Win
With illustrations from Andrew Pinder

ISBN: 978-1-84543-662-9

Printed in China by 1010 Printing International Ltd.

2 4 6 8 10 9 7 5 3 1

365 Mindful Days to Colour

Bring calm to every day with meditative patterns and mindful affirmations

LONA EVERSDEN

APPLE PRESS

'It is wonderful to be me'

'I am so grateful for all my body can do'

'The only place I need to be is right here, right now'

'My mood is light and positive'

Contents

Introduction 6

Practising Mindfulness 8

Using Affirmations 9

Colouring Essentials 10

How to Use This Book 11

A MINDFUL YEAR 13

January ....
February ....
March ....
April ....
May ....
June ....
July ....
August ....
September ....
October ....
November ....
December ....

Index of Affirmations 380

Acknowledgements 384

Introduction

In today's busy world, we all need to pause occasionally and gain a sense of peace. Adult colouring is the perfect way to do this.

Research shows that when we colour, our breathing becomes deeper, our heart rate slows, our mind quiets down and time seems to slow. Like meditation, colouring allows us to step into the moment, and so helps our stresses and worries to drift away.

Why is adult colouring so relaxing? It is partly to do with the intricacy and the detail of the designs. They encourage your mind to engage fully with what you are doing, so that all of your thoughts are focused on the task and you reach a kind of 'flow', a mindful state that is inherently relaxing.

Colouring also allows you to express your creative side. Each of us has our own take on how to treat a particular design, from the colours we choose to the symmetry and patterns we create on the page. Colouring is immensely satisfying because it is an activity in which we can instantly see progress – in the sense that the picture moves towards completion and in the sense that we become more skilled with each project we undertake. For many of us, colouring takes us back to one of the simple pleasures of childhood. It reignites the carefree joy in doing something that came to us easily when we were young. It is a great way to remind ourselves that there is time for us to enjoy ourselves, regardless of responsibilities we may have and however busy our lives may be.

This book has been designed to enhance the relaxing and empowering effects of colouring. It offers you a beautiful design for every day of the year. Each image has been specially chosen to induce a sense of happiness or calm, and comes with a powerful affirmation. So turn to the page for today, pick up your pencils and start your year of mindful colouring.

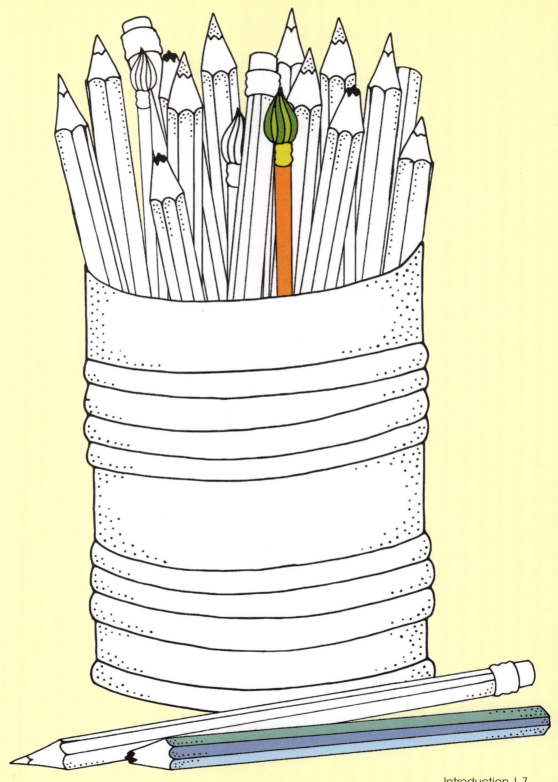

Practising Mindfulness

Mindfulness means 'embracing the moment' – that is, being aware of what is happening right now rather than worrying about the past or the future.

Too often we go about our day on autopilot, barely noticing what we are doing because we are caught up in our thoughts. Research shows a wandering mind makes us feel unhappy and stressed. Conversely, when we engage fully with our moment-by-moment experience we enjoy life more and feel less anxious.

Activities such as colouring, which rest and quiet the mind, are a great way to introduce yourself to a more mindful way of living. It helps to begin each colouring session by spending a few moments being aware of your breathing to calm your mind. Try placing the palms of your hands on your belly. Take a slow, deep breath in, allowing the breath to go all the way down to your belly. Notice how it gently pushes out against your hands, then relaxes as you breathe out. Do this three times, just noticing how it feels to breathe in and out. Then, when you feel ready, begin your colouring.

Using Affirmations

One effect of mindfulness may be that we begin to notice our negative thoughts. Many of us have an inner voice that is harsh and pessimistic. Affirmations are short statements that can help us to change our inner voice to one that is kind and empowering, and thus adopt a more positive attitude towards life.

Each colouring design in this book comes with an inspiring affirmation to transform your day. Some are intended to help you access a calmer state of mind, others build confidence, your creativity or your sense of joy. Over time, they can help you to rise above stress, live in the moment, be happy and realise your potential. Here's how to get the most from affirmations:

- **Say Them Often**
  Repeat the day's affirmation several times for a minute or so. Do this before and after you colour and then at intervals throughout the day.

- **Let Go of Judgement**
  Do not worry whether you believe the affirmation. Simply concentrate on repeating the words to yourself.

- **Wait and See**
  Don't ask yourself if the affirmation is working or making a difference to your day. It takes time for your inner voice to change. Just say it without expectation and see what happens.

Finding an Affirmation
This book is designed to be worked through day by day, but if you have a specific area of well-being that you want to focus on you can turn to the index (see pages 380–383) to find the right affirmation for your needs. In the index the affirmations are listed by subject area so that you can discover the best one to help boost your confidence, focus your mind or inspire gratitude.

Colouring Essentials

How you colour the designs in this book is totally up to you – there are no rules and no restrictions. That's the fun of adult colouring. However, it's best to use coloured pencils because these will not bleed through the page as markers or felt tip pens do. Pencils also give you a high degree of precision, which is helpful when colouring intricate patterns. And you can vary the level of shading by pressing more lightly or firmly, or by creating layers of colour.

There are all sorts of coloured pencils available. It's fine to use ordinary children's pencils, or you can buy artist's pencils. Artist's pencils have higher-quality pigment, which makes them smoother to use, blendable and better for layering. They also tend to have finer points, which is useful for tiny details. Some people like to use watercolour pencils, which are used the same way as a traditional pencil, but then you can brush a little water over the top to create a more painted effect.

Here are some other ways to get the best out of the designs and the time you devote to them.

1. Make Space
Gather everything you need before you start to colour: your pencils, sharpener, container for the sharpenings, this book. You may like to create a dedicated colouring space or to keep your colouring kit in a special box so that everything is easy to find.

2. Be Comfortable
Some people like to colour sitting on the sofa or on a bed; others prefer to be at a table. Do whatever feels right for you, but make sure that you feel relaxed and comfortable.

3. Find Time
The great thing about colouring is that you can do it at any time – you might like to get up early in the morning and enjoy some colouring before the rush or it might be something you do to wind down in the evening. Some people like to colour on their commute… whatever time suits you is fine.

4. Create with Colour
Don't think too hard about the colours you choose, but let your instincts guide you. You may find that you naturally opt for calming colours or inspiring hues that enhance the message of the affirmation – or you may find it fun to make a point of doing this. The choice is yours.

Inspired by Colour
On each colouring page a small segment of the design has been coloured in to provide inspiration for your own creativity. You can take your cue from the colours used or go in a completely different direction. Allow your mood and instincts to guide your colour choice for each image and see how the colours you use change from day to day, or even within a design.

How to Use This Book

This book is designed to give you a whole year of peaceful, mindful colouring, with one beautiful design for every day of the year. Each image has been specially chosen to encourage mindful colouring and comes with an affirmation that complements the design.

Turn to today's page – whether that is the 1st of January or any other day in the year. Read the affirmation and spend a few moments thinking about what that means to you. Then enjoy unwinding, de-stressing and expressing yourself through the power and beauty of colour.

For those times when you want to focus on a specific area of well-being, you can use the index of affirmations on pages 380–383 to find affirmations by topic, whether you need a quick confidence boost or a mantra to help you relax from worries.

A Mindful Year

Whether you are starting on the 1st of January, 7th of June or 20th of December, turn to the relevant page in this book and begin your mindful year.

Enjoy carving out a quiet moment every day through the mindful practice of colouring. Use this time to focus on your own needs and your personal well-being. Reflect on the affirmation for that day – be it about inspiring confidence, promoting calm or expressing gratitude – and use these mantras to help you discover a more tranquil way of life.

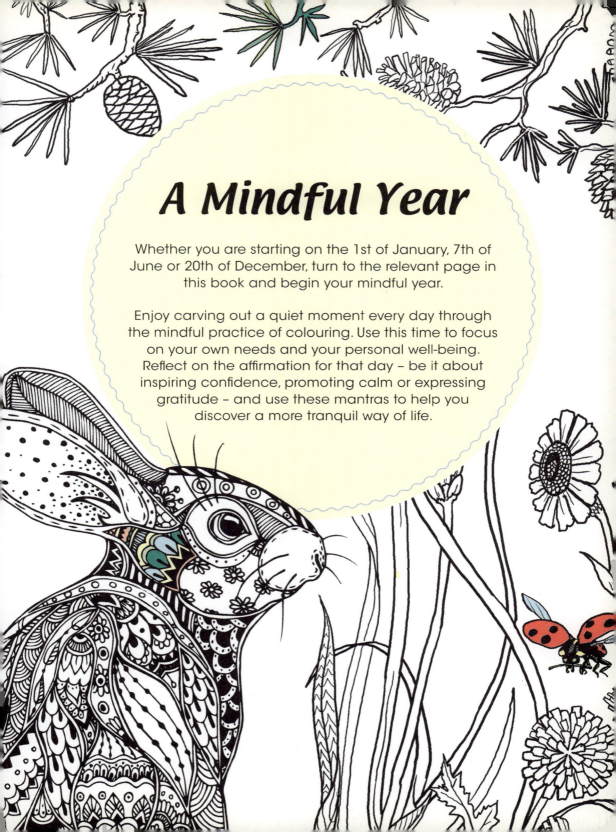

1 January

I choose to be happy.

2 January

Each new day is full of undreamed possibilities.

3 January

Only when I let go do I see how far I can rise.

4 January

I greet each morning invigorated and ready to start a new day.

5 January

I face my fears with the strength and courage of a lion.

6 January

Energy flows through every part of my body, and I feel invigorated.

7 January

My talents are blossoming, transforming my life in unexpected ways.

8 January

Magical things happen when I focus my energy on what I love most.

9 January

Today I set my mind to complete every task with the passion it deserves.

10 January

I know that I am worth all the good things in my life
and that many more are coming to me.

11 January

I take pride in both my body and my mind, knowing that beauty is about more than appearance.

12 January

When I am feeling down, I look up to the sky and remember that the world is a big place full of opportunity.

13 January

My happiness is my responsibility and no one else's.

14 January

There is always a way through – even when the path seems full of obstacles.

15 January

My community is full of people who have hopes and fears, just like me.

16 January

I am the star of my life and I shine in all I do.

17 January
Every day opens a door to new adventures.

18 January

I accept with thanks the small gifts that others offer me – a smile, a helping hand, a sympathetic ear.

19 January

I sail my own way, however choppy the waves may be.

20 January

The independent, creative spirit of Aquarius the water-carrier flows through me.

21 January

I have clear goals in mind and I work hard to achieve them.

22 January

I glow with contentment and good health.

23 January

I release old grudges and open my heart to compassion and understanding.

24 January

My inner self is calm and peaceful.

25 January

I forgive the past and move on from it.

26 January

I am as unique and beautiful as a snowflake.

27 January

Today I carry kindness in my heart and express it through my voice;
I speak as sweetly as the birds sing.

28 January

When I don't know where to start I remember that starting anywhere is better than not starting at all.

29 January

I approach my day with an attitude of gratitude.

30 January

I trust my instincts and follow my heart.

31 January

I conserve my energy for when I need it most.

1 February
The harsher the winds that buffet me, the deeper my roots grow.

2 February

Through forgiveness comes freedom.

3 February

I have the wisdom to know when to keep my own counsel.

4 February

Just as every oak tree grows from an acorn, so each great achievement starts from small beginnings.

5 February

I use my intelligence to come up with innovative ideas. I am a creative thinker.

6 February

My instincts are my guiding light in everything that I do.

7 February

I have the courage to believe in the beauty of my dreams.

8 February

Every day I take time to pause and reflect on all the wonderful things in my life.

9 February

Focusing on each breath, I find the stillness within myself.

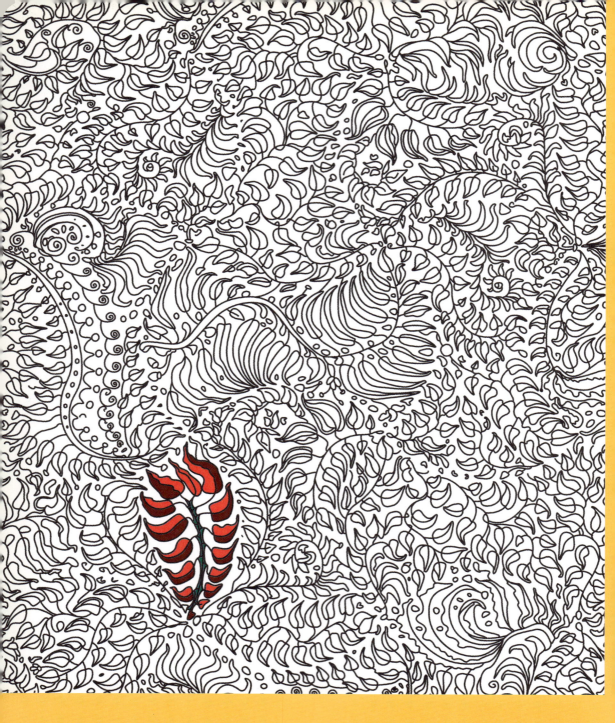

10 February

I celebrate the beauty in every exquisite detail of our world, from a falling leaf to the shape of a smile.

11 February

Like the butterfly, I am free to follow my dreams.

12 February

I have broken free from old habits and I am moving on in my life.

13 February

Today I am positive in everything I think, say and do.

14 February

I am open to the unknown and accept that some outcomes are outside of my control.

15 February

Everywhere I look, I see the miracle of life.

16 February

I keep my cool however heated others become.

17 February

I am the embodiment of grace.

18 February
I am protected and safe.

19 February

Like Pisces the fish, I can swim with the current or against it,
and I make the most of any situation I find myself in.

20 February

Whatever challenges the day brings, I can handle them.

21 February
I bring a sense of spaciousness to my day.

22 February

I stay in the present moment, knowing that it is filled with riches.

23 February

I nurture my body and soul with deep, meaningful rest.

24 February

I observe my emotions calmly, as if through the dispassionate lens of the camera.

25 February

I welcome the sun into my day and allow its healing light to infuse everything that I do.

26 February

Today, a river of creative energy flows within me unleashing a torrent of great ideas.

27 February

Even in difficult times, there is always a beacon of light guiding me forwards.

28 February

I treat my body with kindness at all times.

29 February

I embrace new opportunities with excitement.

1 March

I am a natural decision maker; I make the right choices at the right time.

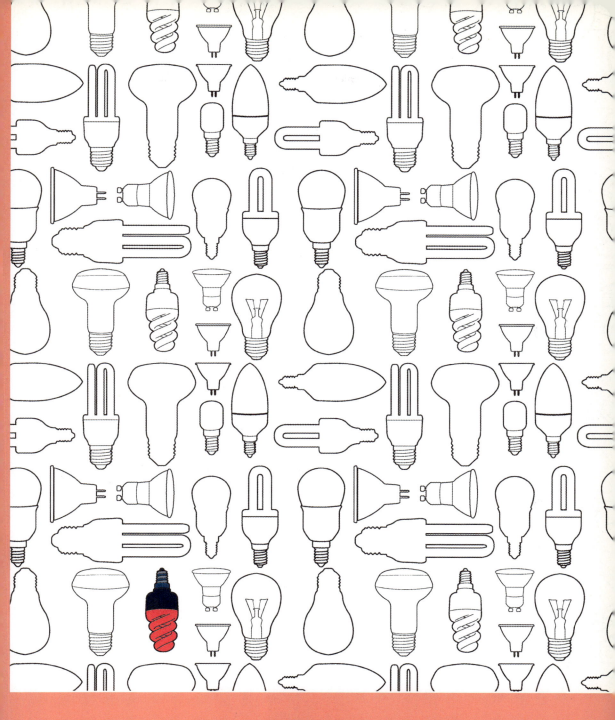

2 March

I believe it and then achieve it!

3 March

The key to realising my potential is confidence in my own abilities.

4 March

I leave my work at work; at home, I embrace relaxation.

5 March

I take a little time each day to daydream.

6 March

I live in harmony with those around me.

7 March

I honour the joy of life; I allow it to transport me to happier places.

8 March

My breath is my anchor; at any time I can use it to reconnect to the present moment.

9 March

I make the most of life's sweetest moments.

10 March

I am always open to new ideas.

11 March

Every decision I make creates exciting new possibilities in my life.

12 March

I welcome times of solitude and enjoy my own company.

13 March

I am happy when others succeed, knowing that there is enough for all of us.

14 March

I bring serenity to every situation I find myself in.

15 March

Today, I broaden my awareness and notice the positive changes that are already happening in my life.

16 March

I realise I cannot know what the day brings;
I only know to expect the unexpected.

17 March

I maintain a little place of quiet inside myself
and know that I can go there at any point.

18 March

I choose to be with friends who know, accept and love the real me.

19 March

I am at peace with my past, my present and my future.

20 March

I freely express my thanks for all that I receive today.

21 March

Like Aries, the ram, I will throw myself headlong into
the day and tackle all tasks with enthusiasm and optimism.

22 March

My love for my family manifests itself in kind acts and words.

23 March

All the threads of my life are woven together in one wonderful tapestry.

24 March
I appreciate the support and comfort that I receive from others.

25 March

I choose to act with confidence.

26 March

I bring positivity into everything I say and do.

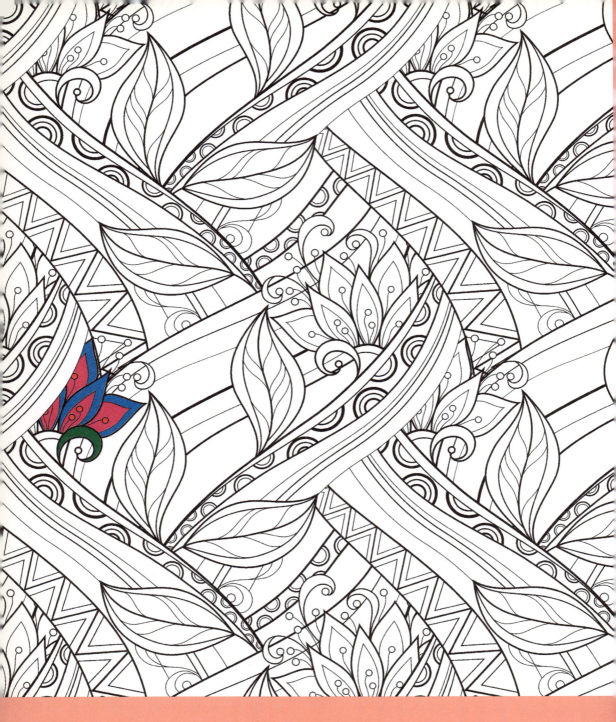

27 March

I am willing to let go of my worries;
I ease myself into a more relaxed way of being.

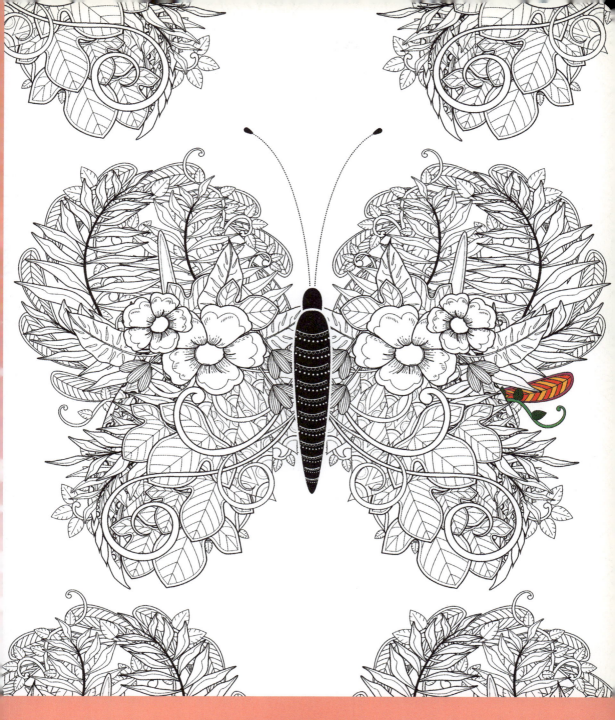

28 March

I embrace the changes that are occurring in my life,
and have faith that they are in my best interest.

29 March

I navigate unknown situations with ease.

30 March

I am not afraid to go against the tide.

31 March

My focus is on what truly matters.

1 April

I am at peace with my surroundings.

2 April
I follow my dreams and take steps to make them my reality.

3 April

I see the good in everyone I meet today.

4 April

Everywhere I turn I see a reason to smile.

5 April

I cherish the time I spend in my home.

6 April

I practise gratitude every day and thankfulness becomes my melody.

7 April

It is enough to be myself.

8 April

My life is rich with blessings and I am thankful for each one.

9 April

I feel invigorated and alive, full of energy for everything I want to do.

10 April

I remember the good things that others
have done for me and I let go of the misdeeds.

11 April

When people speak to me, I listen with mindful attention.

12 April

Just as the lotus flower rises above the water, so I rise above
my difficulties and turn my face to the light.

13 April

I breathe in peace and breathe out love.

14 April

Every moment is a new beginning.

15 April

I have faith in my ability to provide for myself and for my family.

16 April

Amazing things happen when you believe in the possibilities of your imagination.

17 April

I am naturally optimistic; I look for the silver lining in every cloud.

18 April

My cares feel as light as the air; I watch them float away.

19 April

The world is a garden of ideas and I delight in each new discovery.

20 April

I grab every situation by the horns. I have the bravery of Taurus the bull and I stand up for myself.

21 April

I embrace my flaws, knowing that perfection is an illusion.

22 April

There is abundance everywhere; I have everything I need and more.

23 April

I believe that I deserve success and I am prepared to work hard to achieve it.

24 April
I go lightly through my day, trusting that I will find what I need whenever I need it.

25 April

I can open the gate to happiness at any moment.

26 April

I am a fun-loving person with a playful side.

27 April
I wake up feeling happy and full of energy.

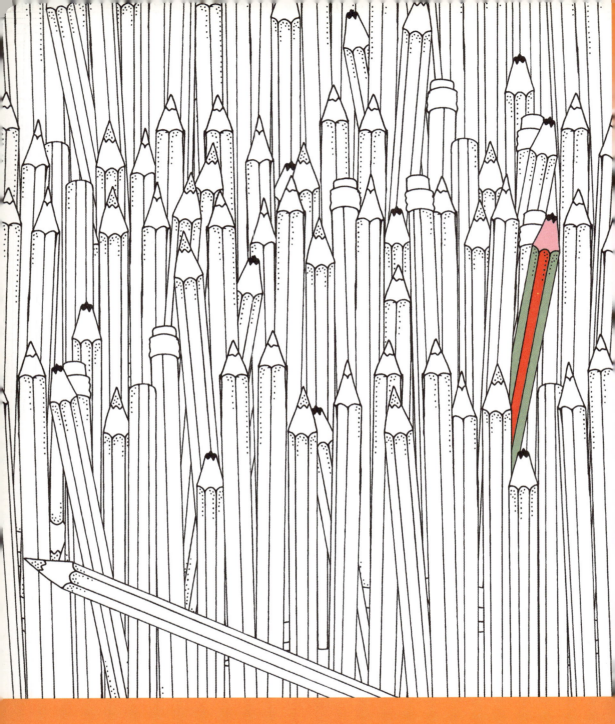

28 April

Colouring is my way of finding a few precious moments of peace.

29 April

Every day I seize the opportunity to learn something new.

30 April
I am strong and powerful enough to make choices that suit who I am.

1 May

I acknowledge and appreciate the support and love of my friends and family.

2 May
My creative energy is a fountain of brilliant ideas.

3 May

Although I may pass through periods of difficulty,
I remember that these are only a small part of life.

4 May

I have the confidence to let my sparkle show.

5 May

I shed old beliefs that no longer serve me.
I am not who I was as a child; I have grown.

6 May

Fear does not stop me; great courage lies within me and I know I can draw on it at any moment.

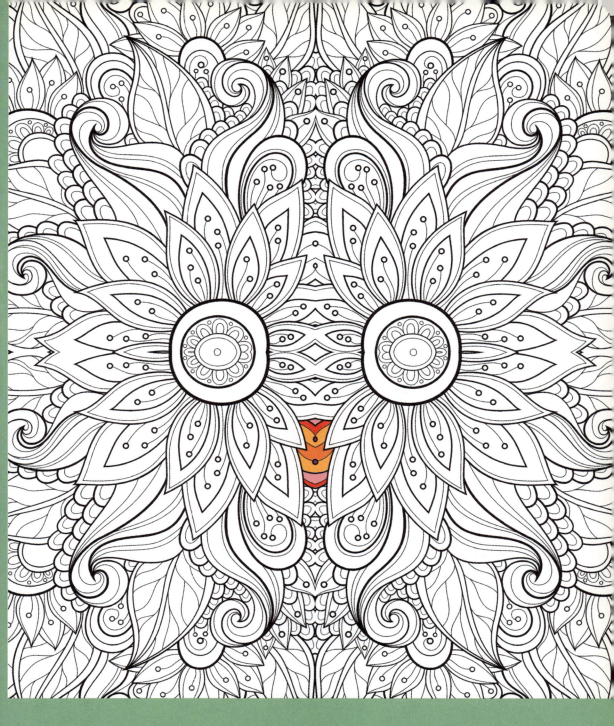

7 May

From my mistakes come opportunities.

8 May

I give my whole heart to my purpose in life.

9 May

On every hour, I pause and breathe.

10 May

Like the bright sunflower, I raise my face to the sun and give thanks for the opportunity to grow.

11 May

I visualise what I want to achieve and make it a reality.

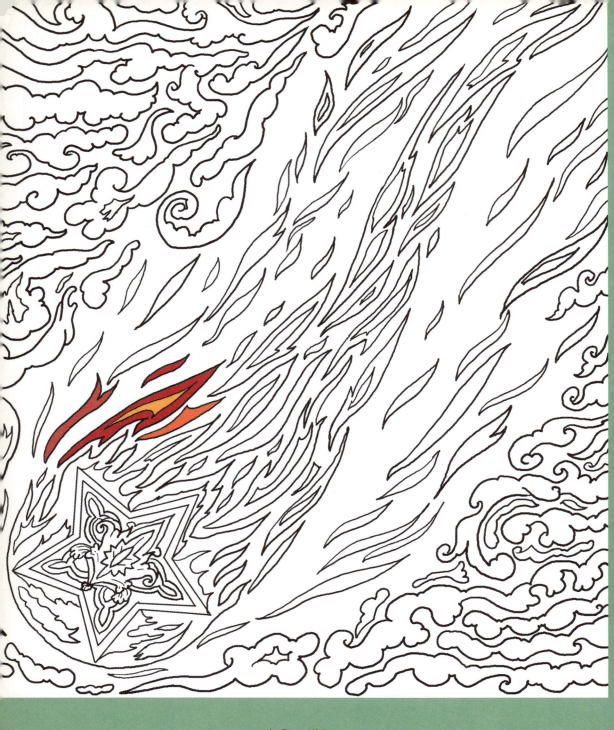

12 May

Today I blaze a trail through my world.

13 May

I create a happy and calm environment; my home is my sanctuary.

14 May

I stand tall and let my inner worth reveal itself.

15 May

Love and peace are at the centre of my being.

16 May

My sense of tranquillity expresses itself in everything I do.

17 May

My inner voice is gentle; I speak to myself with love.

18 May
There is always time for love and nurture.

19 May
I have complete freedom to do what I want and go where I like.

20 May

I am attracting love and affection into my life.

21 May

Like Gemini, the twins, I am able to see both sides of any situation and I am open to new experiences.

22 May

My home is a cosy, safe place to be.

23 May
I take great pleasure in small indulgences.

24 May

I focus on taking one step at a time, trusting that
I am moving towards my highest goal.

25 May

Today I choose to make changes not excuses.

26 May
I love to switch off all electronic devices and spend a few minutes in silence.

27 May

I have the courage to ask for help when I need it, and know that I can rely on my family and friends to support me.

28 May
I rise like the sun, full of energy and brightness.

29 May

Each day I bring a little holiday happiness into my life.

30 May

I am full of appreciation for everything that my body allows me to do.

31 May

Laughter comes easily to me; I make time to laugh every day.

1 June
I always look on the bright side; I am a natural optimist.

2 June

I love the sense of connection that I feel with other people.

3 June

One step at a time is all it takes for me to move along my path.

4 June

When I have something to say, I express it calmly and freely.

5 June

I radiate goodwill to everyone I meet.

6 June

Wonderful things are drawn to me.

7 June

My smile is radiant with joy.

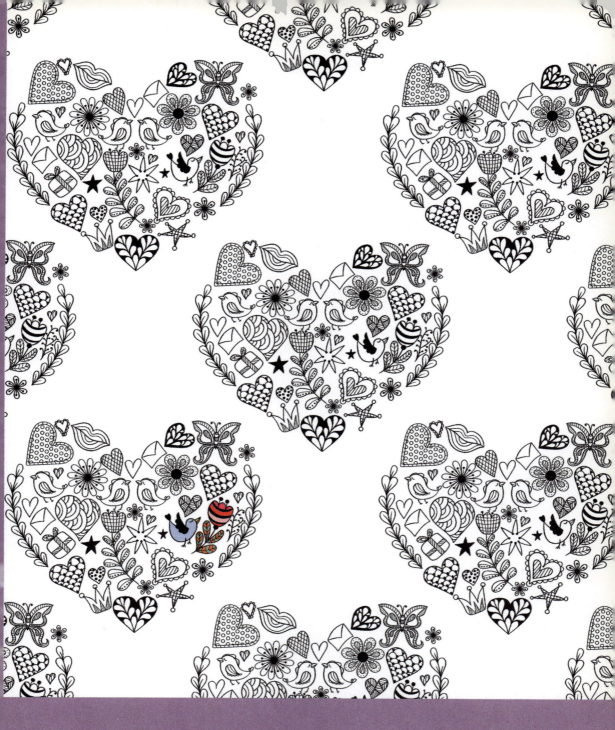

8 June

My heart is open. I give out love and love is given to me.

9 June

I am grateful for all the good things that are sent my way.

10 June

I find happiness everywhere I choose to see it.

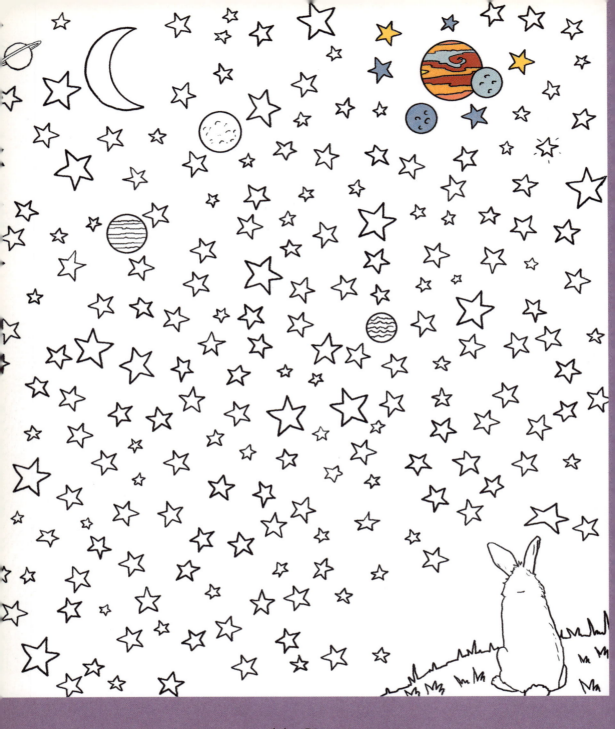

11 June

In times of darkness, I look up at the stars and remind myself that there is always light.

12 June

I am conquering the obstacles that block my
way and creating a happier, better life.

13 June
I do not strive to be perfect because I accept myself for who I am.

14 June

Everything I experience, positive or negative, increases my potential for growth.

15 June

I prioritise the most important tasks of my day and proceed with clarity.

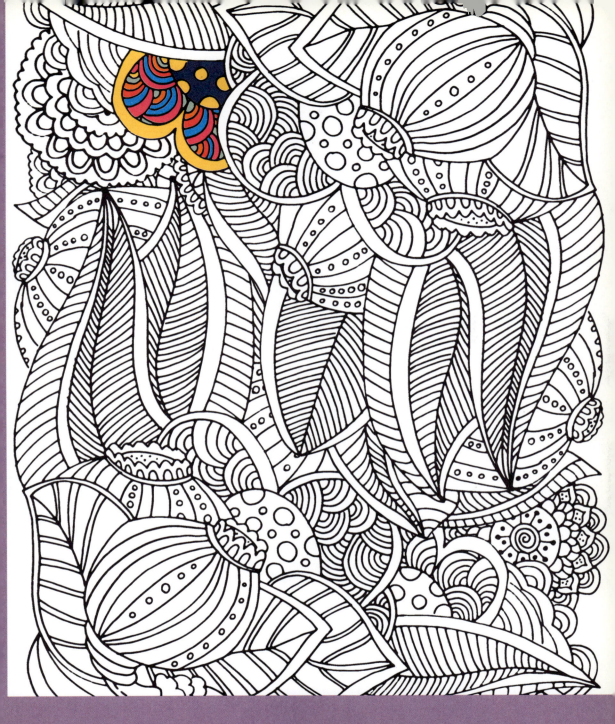

16 June
I am constantly growing in mind and spirit.

17 June

I release my fears and watch them fly away.

18 June

I choose confidence. I have faith in my ability to succeed.

19 June
I am a strong person and I offer support to those around me.

20 June

My confidence is blossoming and I know my future is full of promise.

21 June

Cancer, the crab, is self-sufficient – and the same is true of me.
I feel protected by who I am.

22 June

Every day has its treasure, even if it is hidden from view.

23 June

My relationships are loving and lasting.

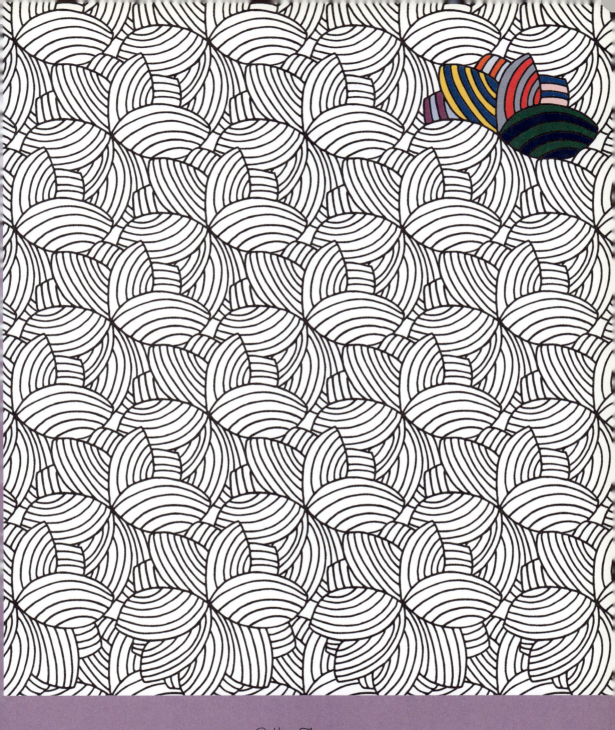

24 June
I can do it. Yes, I can!

25 June

Being cheerful comes naturally to me. I find it easy
to experience the happiness that the day has to offer.

26 June

I choose what I want from life. Everything I wish for is available to me.

27 June

I create deep emotional bonds with my family and friends.

28 June
I am not afraid to take leaps of faith and follow my heart.

29 June

I treat others with gentleness and I am equally tender to myself.

30 June

I relinquish my desire to change the past. As I let go of regrets, I embrace the reality of the now.

1 July

I am radiant. I am blessed with good health and vitality.

2 July

My time is precious and I spend it wisely.

3 July

Today, I bring light into every situation.

4 July

There are quiet places amidst the noise and haste of every day.

5 July

The abundance of the universe is drawn to me in a constant flow of gifts.

6 July

My confidence soars as I learn to appreciate the beauty in myself.

7 July

Inspired by the sensitive deer, I handle conflict with grace and empathy.

8 July

Every act of love or kindness makes the world a happier place.

9 July

All is well in my world.

10 July
I am perfectly in tune with myself and my needs.

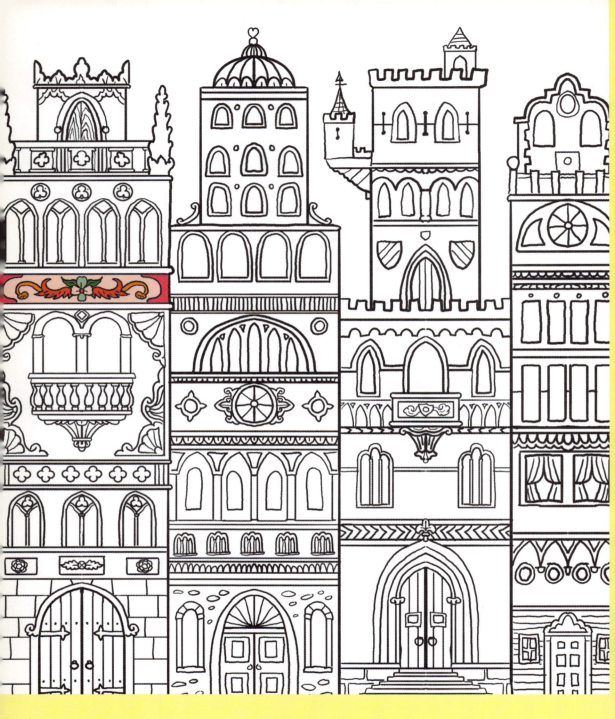

11 July

I am the architect of my own life and I choose to make it magical.

12 July

I am grateful to all those who have been my teachers.
They have illuminated my world.

13 July
Everything is coming together as it should.

14 July

I am nurtured by the beauty of the world around me.

15 July

Inspiration comes to me from many different directions; I am energised by my day.

16 July

Each day I take some time to just be. I allow my thoughts to drift past like falling feathers.

17 July
I have a place inside myself where I can take refuge; all I need to do is breathe.

18 July

There is a deep well of compassion within me;
I draw from it whenever I need to.

19 July
I am a truthful and honourable person.

20 July

I am so relaxed. Tension melts away as I release my worries.

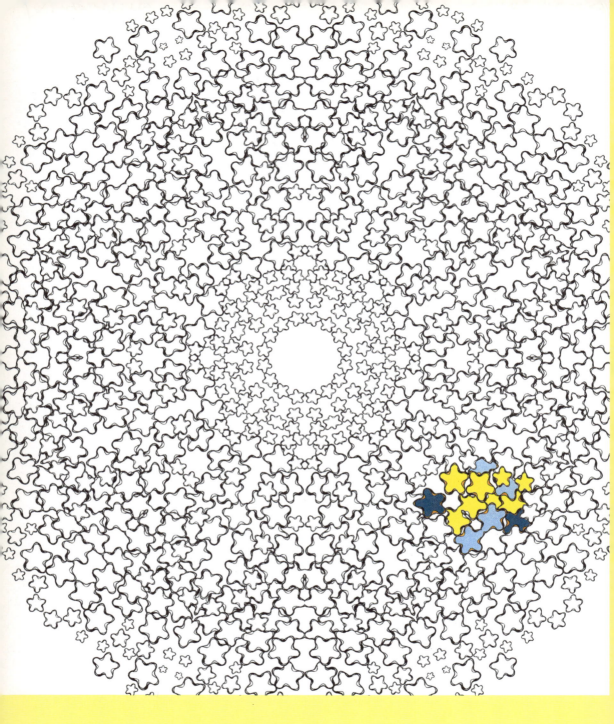

21 July

The blessings in my life are boundless, like the stars in the heavens.

22 July

I am in charge of my own destiny.

23 July

There is a force within me that is as strong as Leo, the lion.
I own that power and it moves me forwards.

24 July
I am organised and in control. My mind is focused.

25 July

My needs are just as important as those of everyone around me.

26 July

My life is filled with love.

27 July

I am flexible in my thinking. I take time to listen to others and learn from them.

28 July

Like a cat, I am astute and resourceful.
I have the ability to adapt to new situations.

29 July

Wherever I look, I see joy.

30 July
I find it easy to work in total harmony with others.

31 July

Good luck always comes my way. I am so fortunate to have what I have.

1 August

Being creative is a key part of who I am. I create beautiful things.

2 August

I allow the possibility that today may be very different than I imagine.
I recognise my expectations are merely thoughts.

3 August

I have a natural wisdom that helps me to understand the truth of any situation.

4 August

I celebrate my uniqueness.

5 August

In the face of adversity, I display the dignity and strength of the tiger.

6 August

I adore my body and know that beauty comes in all shapes and sizes.

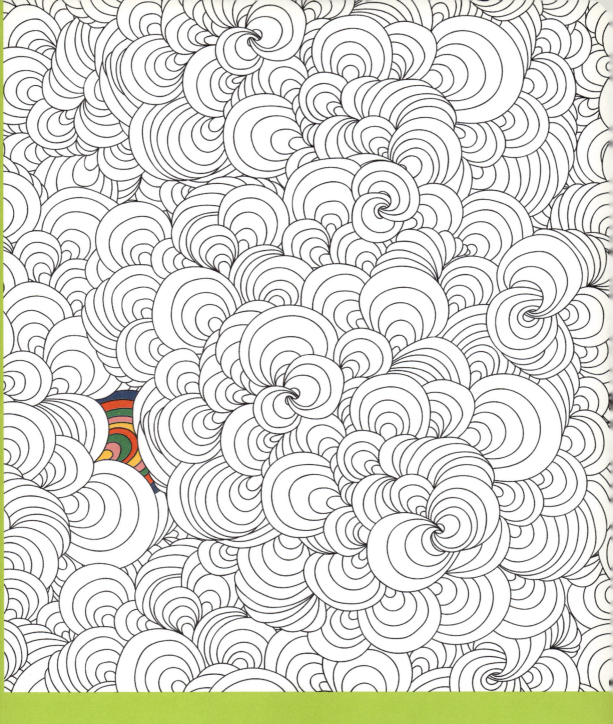

7 August

A sense of peace flows effortlessly through me.

8 August

I hold the key to my own happiness.

9 August

I love the fact that we are all so different,
yet all so wonderful in our own way.

10 August

My ability to conquer challenges is limitless;
my potential to thrive is infinite.

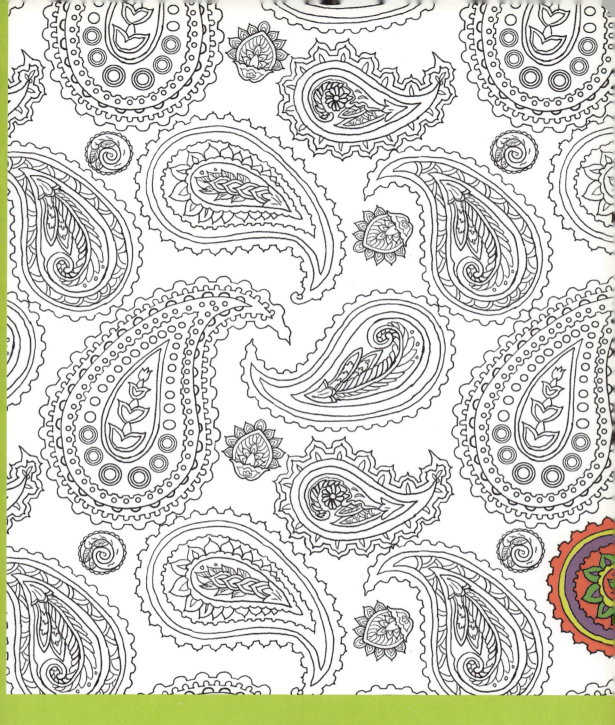

11 August

I am worthy of love just the way I am.

12 August

My life is already transformed; I open my mind and notice the marvellous changes in my everyday world.

13 August
I have love and respect for all living things.

14 August
At the end of the day I embrace deep, restful sleep in a field of dreams.

15 August

There is no limit to my happiness.

16 August

My heart sings with passion.

17 August
My life feels balanced and peaceful right now.

18 August

Today I proceed with clarity and conviction.

19 August

There is such pleasure to be had in the simple affection I share with others.

20 August

I have respect for the deep wisdom that lies within me.
When I receive a flash of inspiration, I act on it.

21 August

Healing energy is flowing through me.

22 August

Everything I undertake bears fruit in a beautiful way.

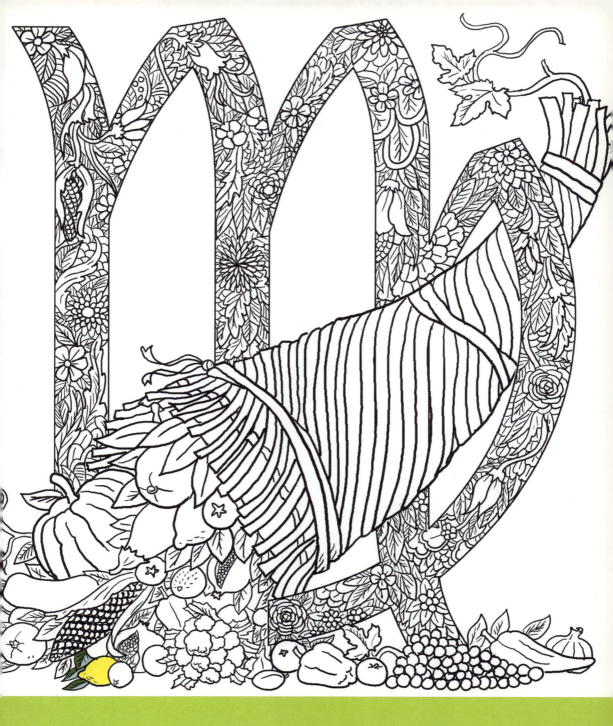

23 August

Today I honour the warmth and generosity of the maiden Virgo by being a kind and thoughtful friend.

24 August

I am grateful to belong to such a wonderful community of people. We look out for each other.

25 August

A little time to let my mind wander allows my creativity and imagination to flourish.

26 August
Life is sweet. Life is full of wonder. My dreams can come true.

27 August

I shape my own future.

28 August

Every day I create a sense of beauty in my life.

29 August

I am working to achieve the results that I want.

30 August
I know that I can go higher and then higher still.

31 August

I see beauty in my friends, my colleagues and in all those around me.

1 September

My calm approach means that potential conflicts become productive discussions.

2 September

I am happy, vital, enthusiastic – and glad to be alive!

3 September

I maintain my equilibrium in whatever storms the day may bring.

4 September

Thank you world, for all that you give me and all that you are.

5 September

I feel the love of those who are no longer with me and am comforted.

6 September.

I listen to those I can trust.

7 September

I nurture my creative self by doing something artistic every day.

8 September

I live in harmony with the world around me.

9 September

Like the seahorse, I hold my place and remain calm, even with turbulent currents around me.

10 September

At any moment I can tap into the source of great energy that is within me and feel revitalised and strong.

11 September

Life is full of adventure. There are always new things to try and new places to go.

12 September

I chart my way across clear waters. I am on course.

13 September

When I nurture my ideas, I see them grow.

14 September

My work fulfils me and I am good at what I do.

15 September

When I want something to happen, I express my desire for it and I trust that it will all unfold before me.

16 September

I am highly productive in every area of my life.

17 September

**Although I may be working hard below the surface,
I present a serene vision of myself to the world.**

18 September

I treat myself with the loving kindness and gentle forgiveness that I deserve.

19 September

All I have to do to make today perfect is smile!

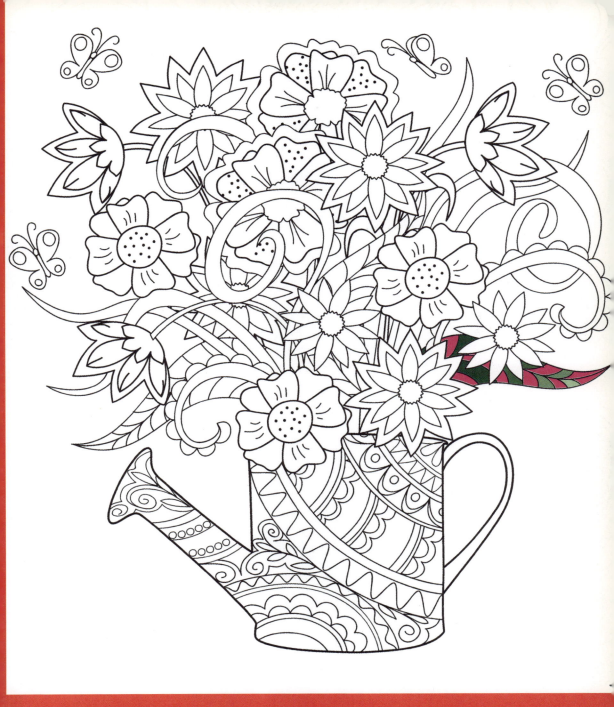

20 September

Having happy thoughts brings more joy into my life.

21 September

My life is filled with magic. My wishes are manifesting into reality.

22 September

Learning new things is important to me;
I love to feed my mind with knowledge.

23 September

Libra, the scales, are a picture of fairness and balance. Today I will be just and even-handed in my dealings with others.

24 September

I have a logical mind; I am able to come up with clear solutions to any problems that I face.

25 September

I create a sense of home and belonging wherever I go.

26 September

I am thankful for the prosperity and abundance in my life.

27 September

I recognise what brings me true delight and make room for it in my life.

28 September

I allow my doubts to be washed away by a wave of self-belief.

29 September
I express my artistic side in all that I do.

30 September

I have the confidence to show the real me;
I do not need to hide behind a mask.

1 October

I have beautiful things in my home.
I make sure to have beauty around me.

2 October

Everything is under control; I achieve my targets one by one.

3 October

I have faith that life is taking me in the right direction.

4 October

Positive energy flows through my body, bringing joy to every step I take.

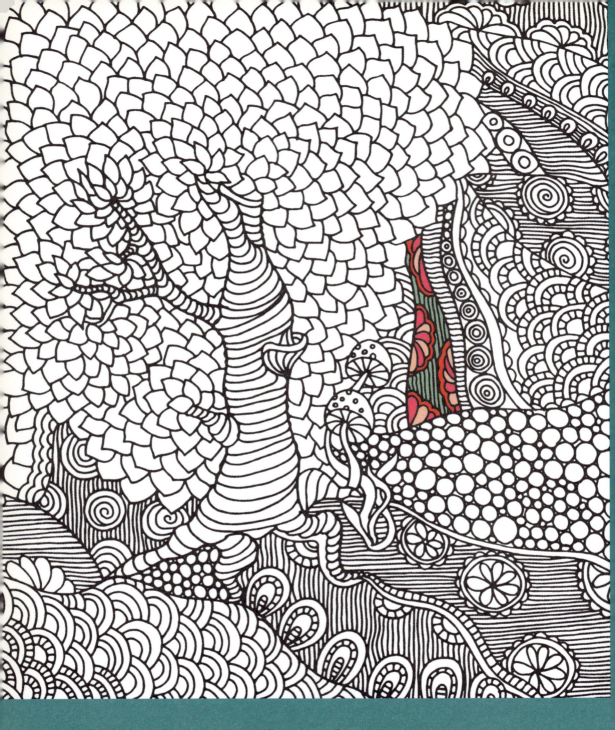

5 October

I gather strength from my roots and keep on growing.

6 October

I have the freedom to go my own way, whatever others may do.

7 October

The unconditional love I receive is a wonderful gift in my life.

8 October

Everything I need comes to me at the right time.

9 October

I am an optimistic person and always carry hope with me.

10 October

I have patience with my family and friends, and acknowledge the love that lies behind their actions.

11 October

One day at a time is enough for me. There is no rush.

12 October

A little bit of nothing time makes me happy.

13 October

Boundless energy is available for me to draw on.

14 October

I unstintingly share the joys in my life with everyone around me.

15 October
I send kind thoughts to all those who need them.

16 October

I am connected to my inner self.
Everything I do reflects the beautiful person I am.

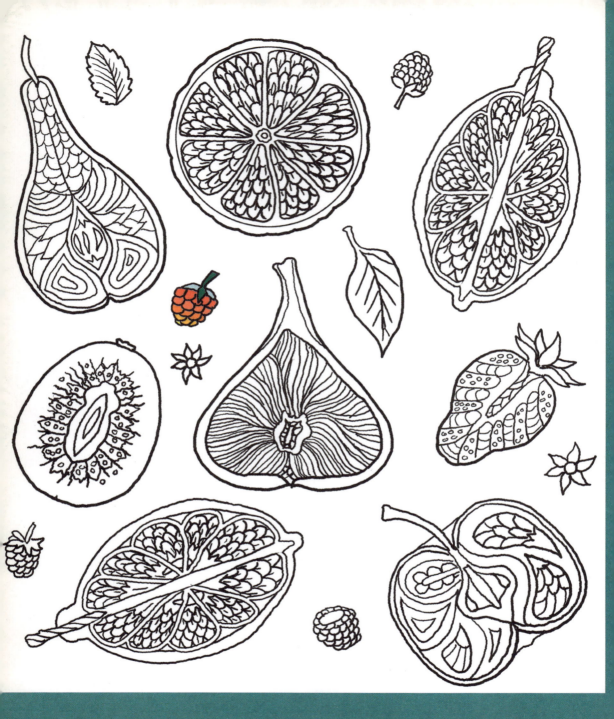

17 October

All my hopes and dreams are coming to fruition.

18 October

I nourish my body with good food, exercise and plenty of rest.

19 October

In all that I do, I am sowing the seeds of my own future.

20 October

I invite my intuitive self to take charge. I value my instincts.

21 October

Today's gift is absolute clarity of mind. I see everything clearly.

22 October

I love the way I look today.

23 October

The dynamic, passionate energy of Scorpio,
the scorpion, is my driving force today.

24 October

I invite new opportunities into my life.

25 October

I see the good in others. I attract positive people into my life.

26 October

Everyone I meet has something to share; the greatest lessons can come from the most unlikely teachers.

27 October

I can let go because I have complete confidence in my abilities.

28 October

I allow others to go their own direction. I celebrate freedom for all.

29 October

Every ending is also a new beginning.

30 October

I drink deeply of life's rich experiences.

31 October

I am patient and resilient; I get what I want.

1 November

I choose to do my best. I do not need to compete with others.

2 November

I willingly go with the flow of life.

3 November

I embrace who I am and all my imperfections.

4 November
My fears are drifting away. I am full of hope.

5 November

Every day I wake with a sense of excitement.

6 November

Life is about more than work and money; I take time out to enjoy myself.

7 November

I am moving forwards – I am on my way to the life of my dreams.

8 November

I draw inspiration from the incredible beauty of the natural world.

9 November

Loyalty is part of who I am. I show how much I value those I love.

10 November

I have nothing to prove: I am who I am.

11 November

I will make peace with those who have been a source of conflict to me.

12 November

I take good care of myself. I am self-sufficient.

13 November

My ability to adapt to new circumstances is remarkable; I embrace the natural transitions that are occurring in my life.

14 November

I have great patience. I trust that everything is unfolding in the right way.

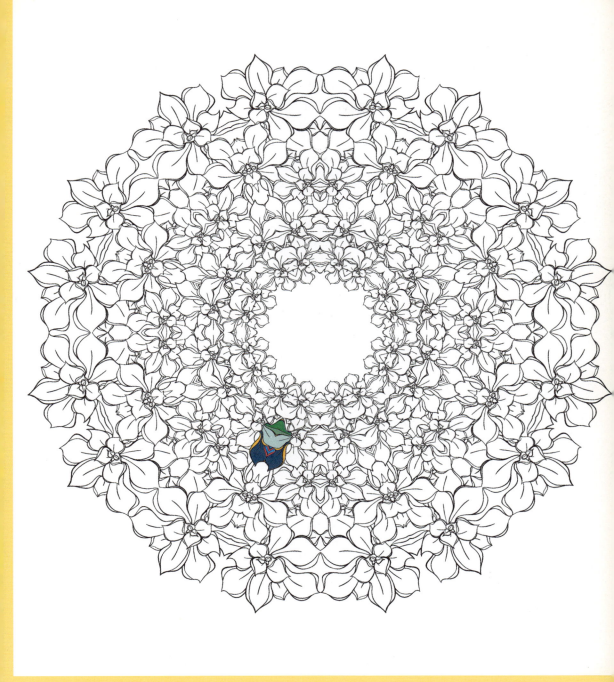

15 November

I release the urge to judge and criticise others
and accept people the way they are.

16 November

Each moment is precious. I organise my life so that I have time to do what is important to me.

17 November

I open my arms wide and say 'yes' to the day
and all the experiences that are in store for me.

18 November

I choose cooperation when working with others.
Although I value my own achievements, I love being part of a team.

19 November

I am richly rewarded for my talents.

20 November

There is a rich and beautiful pattern to my life.
I see the good in what I am doing.

21 November

I move with grace and ease in every step.

22 November

Like Sagittarius, the sharp-eyed archer,
I aim high and true in everything that I undertake.

23 November

I acknowledge the many great qualities that I possess.

24 November

My troubles are melting away, like snowflakes in the sunshine.

25 November

I take care of the things I can control and trust that the rest will take care of itself.

26 November

I love who I am now and recognise
that I am always learning and developing.

27 November
I emanate contentment and calm.

28 November

What I do is worthwhile. I make a difference to the world.

29 November

I create my own opportunities and I persevere until I achieve my aim.

30 November

I love to explore and seek out the many adventures life has to offer.

1 December

There is beauty in even the smallest things.
I am so fortunate to experience it.

2 December

Even in the darkest days, there is hope and the promise of change.

3 December

However challenging my day, there is always time
to step away and savour a moment of peace.

4 December

Success is blooming in all aspects of my life.

5 December

I am completely satisfied with who I am.

6 December

I am in control of my life and choose the direction I travel in.

7 December

I am a master of versatility. I adapt to new circumstances with ease.

8 December

The world is a beautiful place; I am lucky to be here.

9 December

When I feel overwhelmed, I allow myself time for rest and recuperation.

10 December

Each day, I take a moment to check in with
my body and my own needs. I nurture myself.

11 December

I feel completely secure at all times.

12 December

I have fun and appreciate the joys of life.

13 December

I am a flexible thinker – I am always able to look at situations from a new angle.

14 December

Forgiveness is a gift and I know that I am deserving of it.

15 December

Every day, I simplify my life to focus on the things that matter most.

16 December

I respect others and they respect me.

17 December

My inner wisdom lights my way.

18 December

I am true to myself.

19 December

I get what I want from life because I communicate my needs clearly.

20 December

I belong! I feel so happy about my place in the world.

21 December

When I am thankful for what I have, my worries lessen or disappear.

22 December

Inspired by Capricorn, the mountain goat,
I am sure of my footing and I persevere.

23 December

I am content with my present and full of hope for the future.

24 December

What goes around comes around. I do good in
the world and I receive good back many times over.

25 December

Joy illuminates my day.

26 December

My life is a perfect balance between
doing and being, giving and receiving.

27 December

I give myself the space I need to grow.

28 December

The sweetest things in life are given freely and gladly.

29 December

I am friendly and playful, and do not take myself too seriously.

30 December

I honour my own needs.

31 December

I am moving into a more joyous way of living.

Index

A

acceptance
18 January
14 February
18 March
13 June
15 November

achievements
21 January
4 February
2 March
23 April
11 May
29 August
2 October
18 November

adaptation
28 July
13 November
7 December

adventures
17 January
11 September
30 November

appreciation
24 March
1, 30 May
6 July
12, 28 December

aspirations
7, 11 February

awareness
15 March

B

balance
17 August
23 September
26 December

beauty
11, 26 January
10 February
6, 14 July
6, 28, 31 August
1, 16 October
8, 20 November
1, 8 December

bravery
5 January
7 February
20 April
6, 27 May

C

calm
24 January
9, 16, 23, 24 February
5, 8, 12, 14, 17, 19 March
9, 13, 15, 16, 26 May
4 June
4, 16, 17 July
7 August
1, 9, 17 September
11, 12 October
27 November
3 December

clarity
15 June
18 August
21 October

compassion
23 January
18 July

confidence
1, 2, 3, 7, 9, 16, 19, 20, 21, 26 January
3, 6, 11, 19, 20, 26 February
1, 2, 3, 21, 25, 30 March
20, 24, 30 April
4, 6, 12, 19, 24 May
6, 18, 20, 21, 24, 25 June
6, 24 July
22, 29, 30 August
12, 13, 14, 15, 16, 21, 24, 30 September
2, 3, 6, 8, 17, 19, 27, 29, 31 October
1, 10, 17, 22, 28 November
4, 5, 6, 7, 11, 19 December

conflict
7 July
1 September
11 November

contentment
22 January
9, 10, 11, 13, 22 July
12, 17 August
8, 12, 16, 19, 26 September
8, 11, 12, 21 October
2, 6, 10, 19, 20, 23, 27 November
4, 5, 6, 8, 11, 23, 26 December

courage
5 January
7 February
20 April
6, 27 May

creativity
20 January
5, 18 February
2 May
1, 25 August
7, 29 September

D

decision making
1, 11 March

determination
19, 21 January
1, 13, 20 February
21 March
20 April
11 May
24 June
27, 29, 30 August
13, 15, 24 September
19 October

difficult times, coping with
12, 14, 15, 19, 25, 28 January
1, 12, 14, 19, 20, 23, 27 February
16, 17, 28, 29 March
10, 12, 14 April
3, 7, 9 May
3, 11, 22, 30 June
7, 21 July
5, 10 August
1, 3, 9, 24, 28 September
24 November
2, 9, 15 December

380 | Index

dreams
  7, 11 February
  5 March
  2 April
  14, 16 August
  28 September
  17 October
  7 November

E
emotions
  24 February
  27 June
energy
  6, 8, 31 January
  18 February
  9, 27 April
  2, 28 May
  15 July
  21 August
  10 September
  4, 13, 23 October
expectations
  16 March
  2 August
experiences
  21 May
  14, 25 June
  30 October
  17 November
  1 December

F
family
  16 February
  4, 6, 22, 23, 24 March
  3, 5, 10, 11, 15 April
  1, 27 May
  23, 27 June
  27 July
  24 August
  23 September
  10 October
  11 November
fears
  5, 15 January
  14 February
  30 March
  6 May
  17, 28 June
  4 November
flaws
  21 April
forgiveness
  25 January
  2 February
  18 September
  14 December
friendship
  18, 23 January
  2, 16 February
  13, 18, 24 March
  3, 10, 11 April
  1, 27 May
  2, 5, 19, 23, 27, 29 June
  7, 27, 30 July
  23, 24, 31 August
  23 September
  10, 14, 15, 25,
    26, 28 October
  11, 15, 18 November
  16 December

G
goals
  21 January
  24 May
grace
  17 February
  7 July
  21 November
gratitude
  7, 10, 12, 18, 29 January
  8, 10, 15, 21 February
  7, 9, 20 March
  4, 5, 6, 8, 14, 22 April
  10 May
  9, 12, 14, 22, 26 June
  1, 2, 5, 12, 31 July
  24 August
  2, 4, 26 September
  7 October
  19 November
  1, 21 December
grudges
  23 January

H
happiness
  1, 13 January
  7, 13 March
  4, 25, 27 April
  13, 29, 31 May
  5, 8, 10, 25 June
  21, 29 July
  8, 15, 26 August
  2, 20 September
  4, 14 October
  20 December
harmony, living in
  6 March
  30 July
  8 September
health
  22 January
  1 July
help, asking for
  18 January
  27 May
home
  4 March
  5 April
  13, 22 May
  25 September
  1 October
honour
  7 March
  19 July
  23 August
  30 December

I
imagination
  16 April
  25 August
imperfections
  3 November
indulgences
  23 May
inner self
  24 January
  16, 20 October

inspiration
  15 July
  20 August
  8 November
instincts
  30 January
  6 February
  20 October
intelligence
  5 February
invigoration
  4, 6 January
  9 April

J
joy
  7 March
  7 June
  29 July
  20 September
  4, 14 October
  12, 25, 31 December

K
kindness
  27 January
  28 February
  8 July
  23 August
  18 September
  15 October
knowledge
  22 September

L
laughter
  31 May
letting go
  3 January
  10 April
  30 June
  27 October
love
  8 January
  13 April
  15, 18 May
  8, 26 July
  9, 13 August

love, love for others
  22 March
  3 April
  20 May
  8, 29 June
  19 August
  9 November
love, love from others
  1 May
  7, 10 October
love, self-love
  13, 16, 22, 26, 27 January
  5, 17, 28 February
  12, 26 March
  6, 16, 17, 26 April
  5, 14, 17 May
  6, 8, 16, 29 June
  3 July
  4, 6 August
  5, 18, 30 September
  16, 18, 22 October
  3, 12, 21, 23,
    26, 28 November
  4, 5, 18, 27,
    29, 30 December
love, worthy of
  11 August
loyalty
  9 November

M
motivation
  1, 2, 4, 9, 17, 28 January
  4, 12, 22 February
  11, 21, 31 March
  29 April
  8, 11, 25 May
  11, 23 July
  27, 29 August
  11, 13 September
  5, 19 October
  5, 6, 16, 29 November
  24 December
moving on
  25 January
  12 February
  10 April

N
needs
  31 January
  22, 24 April
  27 May
  10, 17, 25 July
  6 October
  10, 19, 27, 30 December
nurture
  23 February
  18 May
  14 July
  7, 13 September
  10 December

O
opportunities
  12 January
  29 February
  29 April
  7, 10 May
  24 October
  29 November
optimism
  17 April
  1 June
  9 October

P
passion
  9 January
  18 July
  16 August
  23 October
patience
  10, 31 October
  14 November
peace
  24 January
  9 February
  12, 14, 19 March
  1, 13, 28 April
  15, 16, 26 May
  4, 16, 17 July
  7, 17 August
  17 September
  11 November
  3 December

perfection
 21 April
 13 June
 26 December
perseverance
 29 November
 22 December
positivity
 4 January
 13 February
 15, 26 March
 14, 25 June
 4, 25 October
potential
 2, 3, 12, 17 January
 3, 10 March
 19 April
 14 June
 10 August
pride
 10, 11 January

R
reflection
 8 February
regrets
 30 June
relationships
 6, 13, 18, 22, 24 March
 3, 10, 11 April
 1, 27 May
 2, 5, 19, 23, 27, 29 June
 7, 12, 27, 30 July
 24, 31 August
 23 September
 14, 15, 25, 26, 28 October
 9, 11, 15, 18 November
 16 December
relaxation
 4, 27 March
 20 July
respect
 13, 20 August
 16 December
rest
 23 February
 14 August
 18 October
 25 November
 9 December

S
self-belief
 28 September
 16 October
 1, 13, 23 November
 18 December
sleep
 23 February
 14 August
 18 October
 25 November
 9 December
stillness
 9 February
strength
 5 January
 5 August
 5 October
stress, coping with
 16, 19, 20, 25 February
 4, 5, 8, 16, 17, 27, 28 March
 12, 18 April
 3, 7, 9 May
 3, 11, 22 June
 7, 21 July
 5, 10 August
 3, 9, 24, 28 September
 24, 25 November
 2, 9, 15 December

T
talent
 7 January
 19 November
trust
 30 January
 24 April
 24 May
 6, 15 September
 14, 25 November

U
understanding
 23 January
 3 August

W
wisdom
 3 February
 3, 20 August
 22 September
 26 October
 17 December
work, success at
 7, 9, 16, 21 January
 4, 6, 16, 20 February
 1, 2, 3, 4, 10, 23 March
 15, 23 April
 15 June
 29 August
 14, 17, 23 September
 2 October
 18 November
 13 December
worries
 27 March
 20 July
 21 December
worthiness
 10 January
 14 May
 11 August
 28 November

Acknowledgements

Quantum Books would like to thank the following for supplying images for inclusion in this book:
Special thanks to **Andrew Pinder** for his beautiful and unique artwork: Cover illustrations
Page 12 (lower left and top right); Page 13 (top and right); 1, 2, 3, 4, 8, 14, 20, 22, 26 January; 1, 5, 6, 7, 12, 13, 16, 18, 19, 26, 27 February; 3, 14, 19, 21 March; 5, 8, 9, 12, 16, 20, 24, 25, 26, 29 April; 1, 2, 3, 4, 9, 12, 18, 19, 21, 22, 24, 25, 27, 28 May; 1, 3, 7, 11, 21, 22, 26 June; 2, 3, 4, 6, 10, 11, 12, 17, 18, 21, 23, 30 July; 1, 8, 10, 11, 14, 22, 23, 27 August; 3, 6, 12, 13, 17, 18, 21, 23, 25 September; 3, 4, 14, 17, 19, 23, 27, 28 October; 4, 5, 22, 25, 29, 30 November; 12, 13, 22, 24, 25, 26, 31 December

Shutterstock.com

Alena Dubinets 24 February
Alfadanz 28 July; 31 October
Alka5051 11 January; 9 September
Anastasia Evseneva 3 February; 31 July
Andriy Lipkan 2 June
Balabolka 20 February; 28 September
Big Boy 20, 29 August; 15 October
Bimbim Page 11; 14 April; 8, 23, 30 May; 12, 25 June; 13 August; 5 September; 10 October; 6, 7 December
Bimbim (vitasunny) 20 May
Catherine Glazkova 19 December
Cerama_ama 16, 18 January; 10 September; 23 November; 20 December
Curiosity 16 December
Emila 1 October
Evgeniya Anfimova Page 12 (left); 20 October
Exclusivelly 23 March
Franzi 30 June
Fricke Studio 2 March
FuzzyLogicKate 7 November
Gala Matorina Page 4 (second row right); Page 5 (second row)
Galina Shpak Page 4 (top row middle, second row left, third row left and right); Page 5 (top and third row)
Hanna kutsybala 5 May; 6 August (top left and top right). 9 November
Helen Lane 6 (middle), 17, 23 (middle) June; 14 December
HikaruD88 16 May; 15 November
Imagepluss 10, 27 January; 25, 31 March; 10 April; 7, 8, 25 July; 16 August; 1 September; 9 December
ImHope Page 7; 15, 17, 19, 25, 28 January; 4, 14, 21, 22, 23 February; 13, 20 March; 18, 19, 28 April; 10 May; 9, 10, 13, 16, 20, 24, 27 June; 5, 26 July; 2, 18 August; 22 September; 5, 9, 21 October; 2 November; 3, 17 December
IR Stone 12 January; 19 June
IrinaKrivoruchko Page 1; 29, 30 January; 27 March; 11, 23, 30 April; 7 May; 6 (surround) June; 1, 15 July; 4 August; 2, 15, 27 September; 10, 13 November; 15 December
Ivala 24 January; 15 April
Julia Snegireva 6 January; 26 March; 7 April; 11, 31 May; 18 June; 20 July; 9, 28 August; 11, 16, 29 September; 7, 8, 18, 22, 24 October; 27 November; 4, 5, 8 December
Karakotsya 12 March; 13 May
Kchungtw 6 May
Kochkanyan Juliya 26 October
Kurilenko Katya 8 February
L. Kramer 10 February; 3 April
Lexver 6, 18 March; 29 July
Lidia Puica 28 December
Lolla Lenn Page 8
Lolya1988 17 May
Mamita 28 June
Maryna S 26 May
Mashabr Page 12 (left); 7, 13 January; 15 February; 5, 9 March; 14 June; 12 August; 14 September; 25 October; 14, 17 November
Mis-Tery 7 September; 21 December
Nadezhda Molkentin 13, 14 July; 30 September; 11 October; 18 November
Nuttapol 5 January
Oksanka007 Page 2 (right); 2 February; 14, 15 May; 15, 23 June; 5 September; 6 October; 19 November; 2, 23 December, Page 383
Olesia Agudova Page 2 (left); Page 3; 1 April; 24 August; 28 November
Olga Zakharova 26 August
OlichO 25 February; 1, 15, 16, 17, 22 March; 13, 21, 27 April; 22, 24 July; 7 August; 4, 19 September; 27 December
Paket 9 February
Palomita 11 March; 4 June
Panki Page 4 (top row right, lower row left and right); Page 5 (lower); Page 12 (middle); 29 February; 17 April; 8, 29 June; 6 (middle right), 19, 30 August; 26 September; 7 October
Photo-nuke 24 March; 21, 24 November; 1 December
Rita Gennari 10 March
Roman Poijak 5 August
Sablegear 28 February; 5 June; 9, 16 July; 17, 26 August
Scotch-me 11 December
Sliplee 27 July; 21 August; 20 September; 2, 13, 29 October; 1 November
Son80 29 December
Snezh 21 January
Toporovska Natalila 24 January; 22 April; 29 May; 15 August; 26 November
TotallyPic.com 31 January; 11 February; 28, 30 March; 4 April; 3 August; 10 December
Uni Ula 30 October; 20 November
Uvlek 6 April; 8, 16 November
Vasylieva Yuliya 6 (lower left) August
Vareennik 17 February
Victor Z 9 January
Vitasunny 4 March; 16 October; 18, 30 December
Watercolour-swallow 7, 8, 29 March; 2 April; 19 July; 11 November
YAZZIK 6 November
YoPizArt 12 November
Zelena 24 September; 3 November

384 | Acknowledgements